How To Price Your Product Or Service Using Price Psychology

SADANAND PUJARI

Published by SADANAND PUJARI, 2024.

Table of Contents

Copyright 1

About 2

Introduction 4

Key takeaways 5

Overview of Pricing Strategies 6

5 pricing strategies with definition Part 1 7

5 pricing strategies with definition Part 2 10

Dynamic Pricing 13

Price Skimming Strategy 15

Bundle Pricing Strategy 17

Penetration Pricing Strategy 19

Value Based Pricing 21

Premium Based Pricing 22

Copyright

Copyright © 2024 by **SADANAND PUJARI**

All rights reserved. No part of this book may be reproduced, scanned, or distributed in any printed or electronic form without permission. Please do not participate in or encourage piracy of copyrighted materials in violation of the author's rights. Purchase only authorised editions.

How To Price Your Product Or Service Using Price Psychology

Use Price Psychology To Make A Profit And Never Undercharge Your Value Again

First Edition: Jun 2024

Book Design by **SADANAND PUJARI**

About

Many people are conducting eCommerce business but are they doing it correctly, where's the opportunity, this is where you will learn about different pricing strategies to grow your sales. It has given multiple price changing techniques you can implement on WooCommerce, Magento, Shopify and other eCommerce CMS or custom websites either through Free or Paid Plugins or manually without paying additional cost.

What about the bundle pricing where you create a deal of multiple, similar or complementary items and sell it through coupon or through email marketing strategy? What about priority pricing where you prioritize the old customers or customers who have newly joined or who have bought in specific categories to promote your products?

Choosing the good and correct pricing strategy for your online e-commerce store is vital, you'll have to test mixtures of a few ideas before selecting the best option that will work best. Pricing strategies are an integral part of your business. But, do most people who are starting understand this? No, they don't. Marketing without pricing strategy is useless and you will understand why the same product with the same price but huge marketing has no sales.

Is this a good strategy to base your prices on production costs or based on competitors? How about different market factors that matter or customer value? In this Book, you will learn about different techniques to grow your sales through the roof and getting newly acquired customers.

Introduction

Many times it happens that you have the same products that your competitors have. So how could you differentiate and make your website, make your products stand out if you have unique products? What are the ways you can price them accordingly? That will give a boost to your sales and you can retain your customers. So how to get new customers and retain your existing customers? So there are different e-commerce pricing strategies for every category, for every type of audience that you need to learn and implement.

So it's not like just posting a product and waiting to make a sale. There are different strategies and techniques to get new users and keep existing buyers. Why are people leaving the card after adding the products while not completing the purchase? So there are many ways you can solve these problems through your pricing strategies. Some of the strategies are directly like. For the people who want to make a purchase immediately, some of them can be implemented later in the user funnel or throughout the customer journey. So in these lectures, you will learn about the best. E-commerce pricing strategies to get new customers to increase sales and keep your existing customers. So where to start?

Key takeaways

Hey, guys, so now let's talk about these efficient e-commerce passing strategies. What are the main things that you are going to be learning? So why do you people leave the card after adding products? There are many reasons. Either they have a better option, a better alternative. Someone is offering them a better price or better quality or better pricing strategy. So you need to understand it from the customer journey perspective. How to retain customers. Now, new products, coupons, these are few things to retain customers. Pricing strategy also has a lot of main points that can take care of that. Too many identical products or many options, but different pricing. So is it like you have to have an alternative, like a same product with different pricing, like a product that does the same thing and you keep a variation of that.

And there are other variations that are easy to source, like easy to buy and then displayed in your ecommerce website. What are the best strategies and how to implement them? This is an important one. Whether you are using View Commerce or Shopify or no matter what niche, what category, your website has, you need to learn like you already know the strategy, but what is the best way to implement that strategy? This is something that you need to learn and stay tuned. You're going to be learning it and implementing it step by step.

Overview of Pricing Strategies

Hey, guys, let's explore different strategies, different ways. How you can implement strategies, so before we dive into implementation, how it works, why you need it, let's go through the basic strategy overview. What are the best ways that suit you and what are the multiple ways varying from category to code to audience? A strategic overview, the basic pricing strategy, the dynamic pricing, premium pricing, anchor pricing, bundle pricing cost plus pricing. Competition based pricing of value based pricing, price skimming, and then you have selling or promoting low priced products to sell the high priced products. So it's more about getting the user to register to buy something. Then after that, you promote the high products, then you have penetration pricing.

It usually goes like you have to know what is the depth that your customer can go into. So these are the. Basic strategic overview, dynamic price can change from category to products. Then we have premium pricing, suppose they need extra something that they're interested in, but the pricing is more like you group different products, you bundle it and then you sell it for a lower or higher price. You have competition based pricing based on the input from your competitors or how you think it should go. Then you have value based pricing by skimming, selling low priced products to promote high priced products, then penetration testing the next. And Elizabeth, in the next lecture, we will go step by step and go through the overview of these pricing strategies.

5 pricing strategies with definition Part 1

Pricing strategies overview some best pressing matters to get sales and retain your customers cost plus pricing. If e-commerce businesses achieve a profit margin between 50 to 100 percent. Then. You can make gross revenue on a higher scale, so if your goal is a 50 percent profit margin, then you make profit accounting for the true cost of sales. So it's like you have a cost of 30, you sell it for 170, then you will be making 65 percent. And it will save you around 50 to 65 percent, considering your cost, it could be higher or lower. So what is trying to say is like this is a generic formula that you can implement because many, many businesses approach it like this, like these are our products we want to sell it for.

This is our best price and we want to sell it at that price because the advertising operations administration, different, expensive, they need to take it in consideration. Some people think differently. They think these are different products. They need to price it differently. So some of the costs oppose the advertising maintenance administration. They associate that cost with another product or category. So that's how it works. Then we have competition based pricing, the second one here in competition based pricing. Yet you have different competitors and you compare your pricing with them and then you make adjustments and then you display, OK.

So there are a few of these like you have the same price, but you publish it differently. You use graphics or web development to show that earlier this was priced at this and now it is that all you can say, like this is the best price anywhere they can get. So pricing strategy and the web development or graphics for the user interface part, that is also one thing that you need to take into consideration. Suppose you bought you and your e-commerce competitor both have the same products going for 20 USD. Okay, but they don't have this product sitting on the product page or product listings page of the original product.

Look, I suppose your competitors don't have that, but you add original products and with that, with their beloved you say earlier 45, now 20 USD. Your competitor doesn't have that. So who is persuading the client? Definitely you, because you mentioned the original product there and then you say the earlier price was 45 USD and the latest price went to USD. So who's going to win this customer? Value based pricing, it focuses on figuring out the maximum amount an average customer is willing to pay. So it is not always good for retailing, even though many times it is for many different products, depending on what you are selling. But it is also one of the good approaches when it comes to customized products.

Suppose you are an artist, you are selling artwork, you create paintings, sculptures, and you want to sell it out. You can say you can. You need to figure out what are the if you have 100 industrial customers, what are the top 20 customers? And then you price it accordingly. Like if it sells for 500 USD and you are an artist and 50 customers are paying 50 USD and 20 to 30 people are paying 300 to 500 USD, then you know, what is your value based pricing? So it works on retailing and it works on customer orders. So you need to find out your value based pricing. Then you have prices skimming.

Pricing decreases over time like we spoke in the competition based pricing also. So popular for products like tech that become less valuable or obsolete as new technology can be produced, so these products are natural, like something launched two years ago. Now, after two years, it will definitely be cheaper. But sometimes the product doesn't necessarily have to be a technology product. It could be something else. Fiji, fast moving consumer goods or anything. And after it has a certain shelf life, so after that, the price will go lower. So there are multiple reasons you need to find out how and.

What are the different ways you can price and publish your products in a way that entices your customers, that make it look more prominent, make it look more intriguing, OK, then you've lost your pricing. It is selling products at a loss to entice customers to buy more expensive products. So what you are doing is that you are promoting supposed five USD products and up until that cost you 25 USD and you are selling a bundle for 25 years, the price to price or either a little higher and then you are through the customer journey. You are selling, telling them that, hey, these are also products that you can also buy. OK, so you are basically acquiring the customer to promote your higher products, higher or expensive products.

5 pricing strategies with definition Part 2

Hey, guys, so in part one, we looked at these pricing strategies and the next one in this part, we will talk about pricing strategies that are dynamic pricing, premium pricing and pricing, bundle pricing and penetration pricing. So in dynamic pricing. It can increase or decrease any time, depending on the market demand and the stock you have and considering what is available in the market and considering your future stock, also suppose the next shipment is. Coming, but not there, so you can change this pricing. There are even plug-ins to do that. The stock is very late. It started from 500 or 1000 now. Only 20 or 25 were left. And you mentioned that this is what is left now.

This and people are actually if you are looking for smart plug-ins, there are plugins like when you have a lot of stock at a shorter discount, but it's going to be finished. Show, sure. Show that it will show that the price has changed. So there are many ways to implement dynamic pricing, then premium pricing. This is used to promote and showcase your valuable luxury products or to promote your brand, to place it as a renowned brand and that it signifies the state is definitely branding elements or graphics photography. How you promote it, who is promoting it, plays an important role when it comes to premium pricing, anchor pricing. What it does is like we spoke in the past and also basically it tells the user, like this is the previous price or this is the price anchor point. It could be a benchmark from other websites and how you are selling it.

What is the price that you are charging? You can say that this was the price earlier. This is the price now. OK, and this is how many units have sold. You can also add this in that there that we begin on this day and so far this number of units or total products have been sold out. So this is how you can use and promote products using this strategy. Bundle pricing is rather simple. What you do is you can say that if you buy this number of units of this specific product, you will get this discount, OK, or you will do what you will do is you will get the product to the people because you will get multiple products, bundle them together and set a lower or higher price.

OK, Set said suppose you have 10 different products mentioned separately and then you have a package or bundle package like you had. You can get all these products in this one bundle for this price. OK, you can also put in that description or use the Vegard or put on the product graphics like 75 percent. OK, so bundle pricing can be used for penetration pricing. What happens is like businesses entering. With a new product or a variation of a new product, and you are promoting it at below average prices. So what happens is you will make your name, you will get to increase your user base. You will be highlighting your for better service, and you will also be checking the market depth.

So often you are done with this strategy, and will have a lot of customers. You will know what the market is, Deb, how much stock you need, what kind of stock you need, how to deal with the customer, what kind of customers are there in your audience, what type of audience you want to see and the sorts of products for them. So these are the different strategies you learn in part one, and these are the strategies in part two. So in later, slightly later lectures, we learn about how to implement these strategies.

Dynamic Pricing

Hey, guys. So in this lecture, we will speak about dynamic pricing, what is dynamic pricing, what are the operations and what are the different price sectors? Look, based on a variety of factors, conditions, trends and stock. It is a process of updating your products, prices over holidays, festivals and time. So basically, based on the requirements, it can be done automatically or manually. So it could have numerous factors. It could be holidays or festivals or specific types of customers or demographics, locations where you are trying to reach out to the audience who could be your customers, who can become your customers. Some of the variations of dynamic pricing are market based pricing, competitor based pricing and real time pricing.

Suppose they are new. Competitors who are in the same e-commerce niche and they are seeing the same products as you are. Suppose you begin with a new product that nobody is selling. So there are no competitors. But after a while, suppose two months, three months, there are few other vendors who are selling the same item. So if you have an automated or efficient pricing system, whether you do it manually or not in an automated way with dynamic pricing, you can have it configured that whenever other competitors set this price or higher the price or lower the price, you could have this price changed according to configuration.

There are different ways to sort it out. Dynamic price factors include industry standards, market conditions, the expectations of your customers and the availability of your product. Is this available for that specific set of audience? Is this even available at all so you can have dynamic price factors? But these are the most common ones, there could be numerous others, but industry standards. Is that suppose you have a product, but now there are alternatives of that product, then you have to change the prices. Suppose the market conditions are changing the prices that were high. But now because the market is saturated, you need to drop the prices. Customer expectations. Customer's expectations are changing or the requirements or or the features that they need. So these are the dynamic pricing and how you could use it in your own e-commerce strategy.

Price Skimming Strategy

Hey, guys, in this lecture, we will talk about skimming equipment, strategy, its definition and uses, so some of the advantages of the skimming techniques are that you have to make your product seem more elusive, like for a specific set of audience, you have to create prestige around your product like apples and few other brands. It is proper, properly done by showing the value of your product, by displaying through different ways that benefits the customers and shows your product is unique and makes your product. Or it could be like it has this number of features, but most importantly, how you communicate that because these type of brands, they are good at communicating and tell the people like this is the good quality and you have to make the good quality as well to stand out from rest of the alternatives or products or introducing the USD like unique selling points that your product have disadvantages.

It cannot be used as a long term strategy if you are not considerate about the price conscious than your competitors saturated the market with alternatives. Apple is among the best examples of how to implement the price skimming techniques. Effectively, skimming techniques often work on early adopters who pay the higher price to buy the new or latest product or the best product that is available in the market. So the skimming is not for all the brands or products, but if you could do it right in a good way, then you could make use of it.

Or I suppose if you have a big line of products, then you want to make one product, rather stand out from the rest and just try to use this technique. You can always give it a try another way. Suppose you have products from different brands and vendors. You can show specific products to the customers who have explored or bought specific brands of value before, so this could work on that. Also, if it is not your brand and you sell other brands products, then you could adopt this strategy differently and implement it.

Bundle Pricing Strategy

Hey, guys, welcome back to our new lecture. So in this lecture, you will learn about underpricing its definition and its uses. So selecting multiple products and selling it as a bundle or buying one and getting one free product, same product or it's another complementary product bundle deals can be promoted in multiple ways. So this is called a bundle package or bundle pricing, you can have a coupon implemented or you have a normal product that is sold separately and then you can have a package like a bundle for a lesser price or for discount or something, an offer that could make people feel like they are getting a better value.

Then you have joint bantling; it is when the two same or different products are offered together for one price leader, bundling happens when a leader product is offered for a discounted purchase with only one product, for example, accessories with the form. So suppose you are feeling something, OK? It is a higher value item, and with that you sell. Low value items free of cost. Now what you can do is you can increase the cost of the main product. OK, so when you sell it, people feel like they're getting multiple complimentary items that otherwise will take them more money to spend. So they feel like they're spending it and getting a better value.

Then you have mixed bundling or custom bundling. It is when customers are offered to buy a bundle or separate product service or products or services themselves. Make bundling or custom bundling. About when customers are offered to buy a bundle of separate products and services themselves. An example is when Web hosting offers you registration, they offer you. A domain name, if you're hosting or if you're buying a hosting, then you're offered a domain, so it works like that. You can also apply on products.

Suppose you say, like if you buy 5000 and you're going to see the value items, then the customers will get this percentage discount, OK? So if they buy one product that is of lesser value, they would have to pay the delivery fees or they will not get the discount. Another example is you're buying 120 G.V. hard drives that cost 200 GBP and then the 200 be, it costs you 350 GBP. So most of the customers will consider the 120 that it is a good deal. It fulfills your requirements and you're paying the price that suffices like it is good enough.

Penetration Pricing Strategy

Hey, guys, welcome to your new lecher. In this lecture, you will learn about penetration pricing, its definition and its uses. So basically marketing strategy is used to attract customers. This marketing strategy is used to attract customers who are being introduced to the new product, offering lower prices during the initial phase. The lower price helps penetrate the audience to know the total depth of the market, and it attracts customers away from your competitors and alternatives and brings them towards your product. And you get to know how much depth, how. For the market, what is the value people can provide, it is the key to running successfully.

To get newly acquired customers, you suppose? Advertise, buy one, get one offer after school, after you've gotten the customer of the user base, you can use it later for up sales and promotions. People might shop at your brand website initially, but after you change your prices, they might choose another brand or go towards an alternative. That's like a good strategy to retain your customers through different products and marketing methods. Disadvantage of market penetration strategy is that. It. Might not sustain your sales after a specific period of time, I suppose, when profit is low and.

You need to have customers retained, so you have to introduce other new features or new product alternatives. That's why you use penetration pricing. If there is an alternative available, then your product might be selected. Basically, the main purpose of penetration pricing is that it is used to introduce the market introduced to the market and nor the total market, like how many units of products you need to produce and what is the demand. And you can also use it as a measure of your pricing strategy, so you can always make use of this in your e-commerce site.

Value Based Pricing

Hey, guys, welcome to your new lecture called Value Based Pricing Strategy, your definition and its uses. So value based pricing is making sure that the customers are paying the price for your product, that they feel satisfied paying and the features you are providing are worth the price they're paying or it is worth their reliability and sort of setting the high price and then convincing the customers it is about research, the customer requirements, getting each scores to make the product, and then based on its value and cost, setting the price for your customers and then promoting it.

Value based pricing can also work for specialty products and small audiences that have alternatives. But your products offer little advantage to choose your product by the customer or support it has the variation or suppose it is more relevant to your customers needs or design. It's more appropriate to your customers needs. If a customer feels happy about your product, the value of pricing will be strong in the long term despite alternatives available. The bad economy and this strategy could help in that situation. Suppose you have these primary features or primary design that your customers like, so it will be good in the long term to sustain your product.

Premium Based Pricing

Welcome to your new lecture about premium pricing strategy, its definition and its uses, the price of a product describes the value given some other particulars, like how its branding is done. While the features also play an important part, premium pricing is the strategy used to price valuable luxury or high cost items or promote your brand for a specific set of audience. Definitely. You also have to consider that it is as valuable as you promote it or your audience. Consider it as such and it is durable. Using premium pricing, the goal is to show that the product or brand is renowned or a specific audience.

It signifies a status, an example is designer clothing and accessories brands supports, suppose they sell for higher value, it could be for their fabric or their market ability or the audience. Consider it as such effective use when it is effective, when a new product is being introduced to the market and you want to promote it to a specific set of audience. Suppose they are new buyers or adopters whom other people follow. Suppose you want to promote it to the audience who buy it and other people follow them.

Suppose someone on social media has a lot of influence and they buy your product and they wear it or use it and then other people follow them, then you can place premium pricing products and market it more successful, unique products that want to differentiate their merchandise with higher prices and a quality image. You have to build perception that the product is a luxury product and it is exceptionally exclusive or high quality or exclusive design. The seller wants to create exclusivity by limiting the number of products or total stock available in the marketplace or the product has no alternatives available. So there are multiple reasons and multiple ways how premium pricing could be used.